# The fruit of the Spirit

Patience

Goodness

Kindness

Peace

Faithfulness

Joy

Gentleness

Love

Self-Control

## Amy Brooks
## Jeff Brooks

ISBN 978-1-0980-7543-9 (paperback)
ISBN 978-1-0980-7544-6 (digital)

Christian Faith Publishing, Inc.
832 Park Avenue
Meadville, PA 16335
www.christianfaithpublishing.com

Printed in the United States of America

To Parents

In the Holy Bible, God's Word instructs each one of us to be part of His ministry by using our gifts and talents that He has so graciously given to us and to using them for the common good with a cheerful heart Romans 12:4–8 (NIV).

  With each children's book we write and illustrate, our sole purpose is **to honor and glorify God as parents and kids come together to read and learn about the Word of God.**

Jeff and Amy Brooks
(BrookLand Ministries)

(Galatians 5:22–23)

But the fruit of the Spirit is...

**Love** God with all your ♥
(Deuteronomy 6:5)

# Joy

Shout for Joy.

(Psalm 98:4)

Peace

Live in **Peace** with everyone.

(Romans 12:18)

Patience

Have Patience with everyone.

(Ephesians 4:2)

# Kindness

Show Kindness like the Lord.

(1 Samuel 20:14)

# Goodness

Love your enemies, do **Good** to them.
(Luke 6:35).

# Faithfulness

Serve God **Faithfully**.

(1 Samuel 12:24)

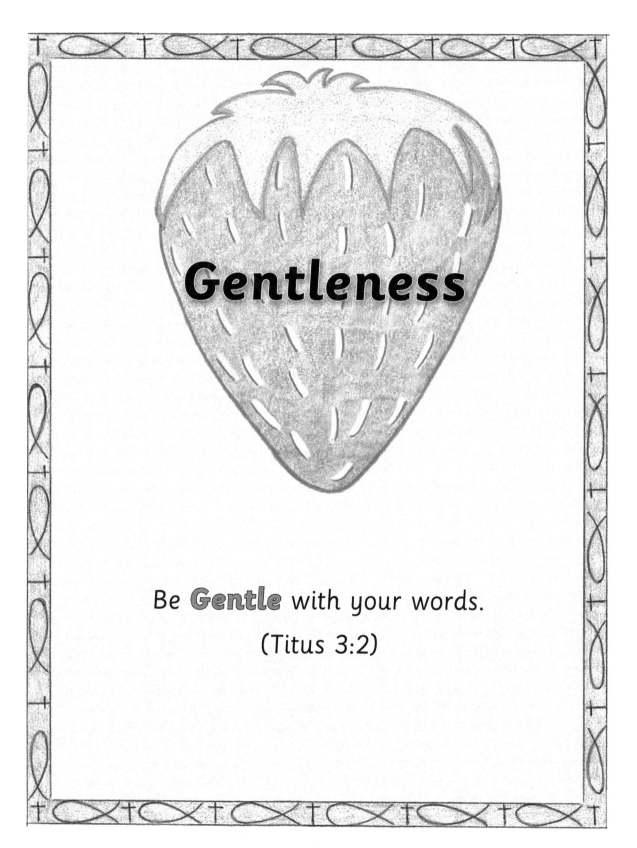

# Gentleness

Be **Gentle** with your words.

(Titus 3:2)

# Self-Control

Always be good, with Self-Control.

(2 Peter 1:5–8)

# Against such things, there is no **Law**.
## (Galatians 5:22-23)

2 Corinthians 4:1–6 (NIV)

Therefore, since through God's mercy we have this ministry, we do not lose heart. Rather, we have renounced secret and shameful ways; we do not use deception, nor do we distort the Word of God. On the contrary, by setting forth the truth plainly we commend ourselves to everyone's conscience in the sight of God. And even if our gospel is veiled, it is veiled to those who are perishing. The god of this age has blinded the minds of unbelievers, so that they cannot see the light of the gospel that displays the glory of Christ, who is the image of God. For what we preach is not ourselves, but Jesus Christ as Lord, and ourselves as your servants for Jesus' sake. For God, who said, "Let light shine out of darkness", made His light shine in our hearts to give us the light of knowledge of God's glory displayed in the face of Christ.

# About the Authors

Jeff and Amy Brooks (BrookLand Ministries) are an extremely happily married couple who live in South Arkansas.

Together, they enjoy living each day for Jesus, and they are privileged to be able to honor and glorify our Heavenly Father through their books and illustrations by teaching God's Word and His life principles to young children all over the world.

As true born-again Christian adults, it is their daily duty to plant seeds and share the Good News, and a great place to start is with all the children of the world!

Our prayer (from BrookLand Ministries) is that each one of our books will bring kids and parents together and point them to God while they spend much needed quality family time together.

CPSIA information can be obtained
at www.ICGtesting.com
Printed in the USA
BVHW022314130421
604820BV00010B/910